The Real Estate Renegade

Unconventional Tactics for Financial Freedom

NELLA BYRAN

Copyright

No part of this should be reproduced without the permission of the author.

© Nella Byran 2024

Contents

Introduction 4
Breaking the Mold 7
Flipping the Script 11
Carving Your Path to Financial Freedom 15
Cultivating the Mindset of a Real Estate Renegade 20
Secrets to Making Money in Real Estate Under the Radar
.... 24
Unorthodox Techniques for Property Promotion 29
Risky Business 34
Rule-Breaking Returns 39
Rebel Financing 44
Disruptive Development 48
Renegade Networking 53
Rogue Renovations 58
Underground Opportunities: Tapping into Hidden Gems in the Real Estate Market 63
Insurgent Negotiation 68
Legacy Building 73
Conclusion 78

Introduction

In the world of real estate, conventional wisdom often reigns supreme. From tried-and-true investment strategies to standard approaches in property development, the industry has long been governed by a set of established norms. However, for those seeking to break free from the shackles of tradition and forge their own path to financial freedom, there exists a realm of untapped potential waiting to be discovered.

Welcome to "The Real Estate Renegade: Unconventional Tactics for Financial Freedom." This book is not just another guide to navigating the complexities of the property market; it is a manifesto for those who dare to defy the status quo. Within these pages lie a collection of innovative strategies, audacious maneuvers, and radical insights that challenge the very fabric of conventional real estate wisdom.

For too long, aspiring investors and seasoned professionals alike have been limited by the boundaries of conventional thinking. But true financial freedom does not come from following the crowd; it comes from charting your own course, embracing risk, and seizing opportunities where others see obstacles. Whether you're a novice looking to make your mark or a seasoned veteran in search of new horizons, this book is your passport to a realm of limitless possibilities.

Each chapter of "The Real Estate Renegade" is a testament to the power of thinking outside the box. From guerrilla marketing tactics to rogue renovation techniques, from unconventional financing solutions to underground opportunities waiting to be unearthed, every page is infused with the spirit of rebellion against the mundane.

But beyond the practical strategies and tactical maneuvers, this book is also about mindset. It's about cultivating the maverick mindset of a real estate renegade—one that embraces risk, challenges convention, and dares to dream big. Because true success in real estate isn't just about making money; it's about creating a legacy, leaving a lasting impact, and building a life of true financial freedom.

So, whether you're ready to flip the script on traditional property investment, carve your own path to financial freedom, or simply embark on a journey of exploration and discovery, "The Real Estate Renegade" is your guide, your companion, and your inspiration. It's time to break free from the chains of convention and unleash the renegade within. Are you ready to join the rebellion?

Breaking the Mold

In the ever-evolving landscape of real estate, success often hinges on the ability to think outside the box and embrace unconventional strategies. This first chapter, "Breaking the Mold," sets the tone for the entire book by challenging readers to discard the limitations of conventional wisdom and explore innovative approaches to property investment and development.

At its core, breaking the mold in real estate entails breaking free from the constraints of traditional thinking and venturing into uncharted territory. It requires a willingness to challenge the status quo, defy industry norms, and explore alternative paths to success. While conventional strategies may offer a sense of security, they often result in predictable outcomes and limited growth potential. Embracing unconventionality, on the other hand, opens the door to new possibilities and untapped opportunities.

One of the key principles of breaking the mold in real estate is creativity. By thinking creatively, investors and developers can uncover unique solutions to common challenges and differentiate themselves in a crowded market. This might involve reimagining the use of a property, finding innovative financing options, or implementing unconventional marketing tactics to attract buyers or tenants.

Moreover, embracing unconventional strategies in real estate requires a willingness to take calculated risks. While conventional wisdom may advocate for conservative decision-making, renegade investors understand that calculated risks can lead to substantial rewards. Whether it's investing in emerging markets, pursuing unconventional property types, or experimenting with new business models, taking calculated risks is essential for breaking the mold and achieving financial freedom.

Another aspect of breaking the mold involves challenging traditional notions of success and redefining what it means to thrive in the real estate industry. Instead of solely focusing on short-term profits, renegade investors prioritize long-term sustainability, community impact, and environmental stewardship. By aligning their goals with broader social and environmental objectives, they not only create value for themselves but also contribute to the greater good.

Furthermore, breaking the mold requires a willingness to adapt and evolve in response to changing market dynamics. In an industry as dynamic as real estate, clinging to outdated strategies and practices is a recipe for stagnation. Renegade investors embrace change, continuously seek out new opportunities, and remain flexible in their approach to property investment and development.

Ultimately, breaking the mold in real estate is about more than just making money; it's about forging a path that is uniquely your own. By embracing unconventionality, creativity, risk-taking, and adaptability, investors and developers can unlock new levels of success and achieve financial freedom on their own terms. As we delve deeper into the chapters that follow, we will explore specific strategies and tactics for breaking the mold and thriving in the ever-evolving world of real estate.

Flipping the Script

In the realm of real estate, traditional approaches to property investment often involve a predictable cycle of acquisition, renovation, and resale. However, to truly break free from the constraints of convention and achieve remarkable success, investors must be willing to flip the script and embrace renegade approaches to property investment.

Flipping the script in property investment entails challenging the traditional norms and exploring alternative strategies that offer greater flexibility, creativity, and potential for profit. Rather than adhering strictly to the traditional model of flipping houses for quick returns, renegade investors seek out unconventional opportunities and approaches that set them apart from the competition.

One renegade approach to property investment involves focusing on long-term value creation rather than short-term gains. Instead of simply flipping properties for a quick profit, renegade investors adopt a buy-and-hold strategy, acquiring properties with the intention of generating steady cash flow and building equity over time. This approach requires patience, foresight, and a willingness to invest in properties with long-term potential, rather than simply chasing after quick wins.

Another renegade approach to property investment is to explore alternative property types and markets that are often overlooked by traditional investors. While residential real estate may be the most familiar and accessible asset class, renegade investors recognize that opportunities for significant returns exist in other sectors, such as commercial, industrial, or even unconventional properties like mobile home parks or self-storage facilities. By expanding their horizons and thinking outside the box, renegade investors can uncover hidden gems and capitalize on emerging trends that others may overlook.

Renegade investors also understand the importance of leveraging technology and data analytics to gain a competitive edge in the market. In an age where information is abundant and technology is constantly evolving, savvy investors harness the power of data to identify investment opportunities, analyze market trends, and optimize their investment strategies. Whether it's using predictive analytics to forecast market trends or utilizing virtual reality to offer immersive property tours, renegade investors are at the forefront of leveraging technology to drive success in real estate.

Moreover, renegade investors recognize the value of strategic partnerships and collaboration in achieving their investment goals. Rather than going it alone, they seek out synergistic relationships with like-minded investors, developers, and industry professionals who can provide expertise, resources, and support. By pooling their resources and collective knowledge, renegade investors can amplify their impact and unlock new opportunities for growth and success.

In essence, flipping the script in property investment is about challenging the conventional wisdom, embracing alternative approaches, and forging a path that is uniquely your own. By adopting renegade approaches to property investment, investors can break free from the constraints of tradition, unlock new levels of success, and achieve financial freedom on their own terms. As we delve deeper into the chapters that follow, we will explore specific strategies and tactics for flipping the script and thriving in the dynamic world of real estate investment.

Carving Your Path to Financial Freedom

In the vast landscape of real estate investment, the journey to financial freedom is not merely about following established paths; it's about blazing new trails and carving out your own destiny. This chapter, "Trailblazing Tactics," is a call to action for aspiring investors to break free from the confines of convention and chart their own course towards prosperity.

At its core, trailblazing in real estate requires a willingness to step outside of your comfort zone and embrace calculated risks. It's about daring to venture into uncharted territory, whether that means investing in emerging markets, exploring alternative property types, or pioneering innovative investment strategies. By embracing a spirit of adventure and exploration, investors can uncover new opportunities and unlock untapped potential in the market.

One trailblazing tactic in real estate investment is to adopt a contrarian mindset. Instead of following the herd and investing in popular markets or asset classes, trailblazers seek out opportunities where others fear to tread. This might involve investing in overlooked neighborhoods with potential for gentrification, targeting distressed properties with significant upside potential, or capitalizing on market downturns when others are fleeing. By going against the grain and swimming against the current, trailblazers can often uncover hidden gems and achieve outsized returns.

Moreover, trailblazing in real estate requires a commitment to continuous learning and personal growth. In an industry as dynamic and complex as real estate, there is always something new to learn and explore. Whether it's mastering new investment strategies, staying abreast of market trends, or honing negotiation skills, trailblazers understand the importance of investing in themselves and their knowledge base. By embracing a growth mindset and constantly seeking out new opportunities for learning and development, investors can position themselves for long-term success in the ever-evolving world of real estate.

Another trailblazing tactic in real estate investment is to leverage technology and innovation to gain a competitive edge. From data analytics and artificial intelligence to virtual reality and blockchain technology, trailblazers harness the power of cutting-edge tools and technologies to streamline processes, identify investment opportunities, and optimize decision-making. By staying ahead of the curve and embracing technological advancements, investors can gain a strategic advantage in the market and achieve superior results.

Furthermore, trailblazing in real estate requires a willingness to think creatively and adapt to changing market conditions. Rather than adhering rigidly to a predetermined investment strategy, trailblazers remain agile and flexible, adjusting their approach as needed to capitalize on emerging opportunities and navigate challenges. By embracing creativity, flexibility, and adaptability, investors can overcome obstacles, mitigate risks, and ultimately achieve financial freedom on their own terms.

In essence, trailblazing tactics in real estate investment are about more than just following a set of prescribed rules or formulas; they're about forging your own path, embracing risk, and seizing opportunities where others see obstacles. By adopting a contrarian mindset, committing to continuous learning, leveraging technology and innovation, and embracing creativity and adaptability, investors can blaze new trails and carve their own path to financial freedom in the dynamic world of real estate. As we delve deeper into the chapters that follow, we will explore specific strategies and tactics for trailblazing in real estate investment and charting a course towards prosperity.

Cultivating the Mindset of a Real Estate Renegade

In the world of real estate, success isn't just about following a set of prescribed steps or adhering to conventional wisdom; it's about cultivating a mindset of innovation, resilience, and audacity. This chapter, "Maverick Mindset," delves into the inner workings of successful real estate renegades and offers insights into how aspiring investors can cultivate the mindset needed to thrive in the competitive landscape of property investment.

At its core, the maverick mindset is characterized by a willingness to challenge the status quo and defy conventional wisdom. Real estate renegades understand that true success often lies outside the boundaries of tradition and are unafraid to blaze their own trails, take calculated risks, and experiment with new approaches. By embracing a spirit of curiosity and adventure, they continually push the boundaries of what's possible in the world of real estate.

One key aspect of the maverick mindset is resilience in the face of adversity. In an industry as unpredictable and volatile as real estate, setbacks and obstacles are inevitable. However, renegades view these challenges not as roadblocks, but as opportunities for growth and learning. They approach failure as a stepping stone to success, embracing setbacks as valuable lessons that ultimately strengthen their resolve and sharpen their skills.

Moreover, the maverick mindset is characterized by a relentless pursuit of excellence and continuous improvement. Real estate renegades understand that success is not a destination but a journey, and they are committed to constant growth and development. Whether it's honing their negotiation skills, expanding their knowledge of market trends, or mastering new investment strategies, renegades are always seeking out ways to elevate their game and stay ahead of the curve.

Another hallmark of the maverick mindset is a willingness to think creatively and outside the box. Renegades understand that innovation is the key to staying ahead in a competitive market and are unafraid to challenge conventional thinking and explore new ideas. Whether it's identifying untapped niches in the market, devising novel investment strategies, or leveraging technology to gain a competitive edge, renegades are constantly pushing the boundaries of what's possible in real estate.

Furthermore, the maverick mindset is characterized by a strong sense of purpose and passion for the work. Real estate renegades aren't just in it for the money; they're driven by a deep-seated desire to make a positive impact, create value, and leave a lasting legacy. Whether it's revitalizing distressed neighborhoods, providing affordable housing solutions, or spearheading sustainable development projects, renegades are guided by a sense of purpose that transcends mere profit-seeking.

In essence, cultivating the maverick mindset is about more than just adopting a set of attitudes or behaviors; it's about embracing a way of thinking and being that empowers you to overcome obstacles, seize opportunities, and achieve extraordinary success in the world of real estate. By cultivating resilience, embracing continuous improvement, thinking creatively, and staying true to your purpose, you can unleash the full potential of the maverick mindset and chart a course towards financial freedom and fulfillment in the dynamic world of property investment. As we delve deeper into the chapters that follow, we will explore specific strategies and tactics for cultivating the maverick mindset and thriving as a real estate renegade.

Secrets to Making Money in Real Estate Under the Radar

In the fast-paced and often competitive world of real estate investment, there exists a hidden realm of opportunity for those who operate under the radar. This chapter, "Stealth Wealth," delves into the clandestine tactics and covert strategies employed by savvy investors to generate wealth in the shadows of the real estate market.

At its essence, stealth wealth in real estate involves flying under the radar and executing transactions discreetly, without attracting undue attention. While some investors may seek the spotlight and pursue high-profile deals, stealth wealth practitioners understand the value of operating quietly and strategically, often leveraging secrecy to their advantage. This approach allows them to navigate the market with agility and precision, avoiding unnecessary scrutiny and maximizing their returns.

One of the primary secrets to making money in real estate under the radar is to cultivate a network of trusted insiders and industry contacts. Stealth wealth practitioners understand the importance of discretion and confidentiality and rely on a tight-knit network of professionals who can provide valuable insights, off-market opportunities, and discreet transactional support. Whether it's connecting with seasoned brokers, tapping into private investor networks, or cultivating relationships with local insiders, building a network of trusted allies is essential for operating successfully under the radar.

Moreover, stealth wealth in real estate often involves employing creative financing strategies and structuring deals in ways that minimize visibility and maximize returns. This might include utilizing private financing sources, structuring seller-financed transactions, or leveraging creative financing techniques such as lease options or seller carry-backs. By thinking outside the box and exploring alternative financing options, stealth wealth practitioners can access capital and execute deals with minimal exposure.

Another key aspect of stealth wealth in real estate is mastering the art of due diligence and conducting thorough research to identify hidden opportunities and mitigate risks. While some investors may rely solely on publicly available information and market data, stealth wealth practitioners understand the value of digging deeper and uncovering insights that others may overlook. This might involve conducting off-market research, tapping into local knowledge and expertise, or leveraging proprietary data sources to gain a competitive edge.

Furthermore, stealth wealth practitioners understand the importance of strategic asset allocation and diversification to protect and grow their wealth over time. Rather than putting all their eggs in one basket, they carefully allocate their resources across a range of asset classes and investment opportunities, spreading risk and maximizing potential returns. This might involve investing in a mix of residential, commercial, and alternative property types, as well as diversifying across geographic markets and investment strategies.

In essence, stealth wealth in real estate is about more than just making money; it's about operating with discretion, intelligence, and foresight to achieve financial success while flying under the radar. By cultivating a network of trusted insiders, employing creative financing strategies, conducting thorough due diligence, and diversifying strategically, investors can unlock hidden opportunities and maximize their returns in the dynamic and competitive world of real estate investment. As we delve deeper into the chapters that follow, we will explore specific strategies and tactics for mastering the art of stealth wealth and achieving financial freedom in the shadows of the real estate market

Unorthodox Techniques for Property Promotion

In the competitive arena of real estate, traditional marketing tactics often fall short in capturing the attention of prospective buyers or tenants. This chapter, "Guerrilla Marketing," unveils the unconventional and disruptive strategies employed by savvy investors and developers to promote their properties in ways that defy the norm and command attention.

Guerrilla marketing in real estate is all about thinking outside the box and leveraging creativity, innovation, and ingenuity to stand out in a crowded marketplace. It involves breaking free from the constraints of traditional marketing channels and embracing unorthodox tactics that capture the imagination and leave a lasting impression on potential buyers or tenants.

One of the key principles of guerrilla marketing is the element of surprise. Rather than relying on predictable advertising methods or passive listing platforms, guerrilla marketers seek to disrupt the status quo and capture attention through unexpected and attention-grabbing tactics. This might involve staging attention-grabbing stunts or events, creating viral marketing campaigns, or utilizing unconventional advertising mediums to generate buzz and curiosity around a property.

Moreover, guerrilla marketing in real estate often involves tapping into the power of storytelling and creating compelling narratives that resonate with target audiences. Instead of simply listing the features and amenities of a property, guerrilla marketers craft engaging narratives that evoke emotion, spark curiosity, and compel action. Whether it's highlighting the history and unique character of a property, showcasing the lifestyle and community amenities, or telling the story of the people behind the development, storytelling is a powerful tool for capturing attention and building connections with potential buyers or tenants.

Another aspect of guerrilla marketing in real estate is leveraging technology and digital platforms to amplify reach and engagement. From social media marketing and influencer partnerships to immersive virtual tours and interactive content, guerrilla marketers harness the power of digital innovation to create immersive, engaging experiences that resonate with today's tech-savvy consumers. By embracing cutting-edge technologies and digital platforms, marketers can reach a wider audience, drive engagement, and build brand awareness in ways that traditional marketing methods simply cannot match.

Furthermore, guerrilla marketing in real estate involves fostering a sense of community and engaging with target audiences in meaningful ways. Rather than simply broadcasting messages to passive consumers, guerrilla marketers seek to cultivate relationships and foster connections with potential buyers or tenants. This might involve hosting community events, sponsoring local initiatives, or engaging in grassroots outreach efforts to build trust and rapport with target audiences.

In essence, guerrilla marketing in real estate is about more than just promoting properties; it's about creating memorable experiences, building connections, and sparking conversations that drive action and generate results. By embracing creativity, innovation, and ingenuity, marketers can break free from the constraints of traditional marketing and capture the hearts and minds of their target audiences in the dynamic and competitive world of real estate. As we delve deeper into the chapters that follow, we will explore specific strategies and tactics for mastering the art of guerrilla marketing and achieving success in property promotion.

Risky Business

Navigating the wild terrain of real estate investment is akin to embarking on an adventurous journey fraught with risks, uncertainties, and unexpected challenges. This chapter, aptly titled "Risky Business," delves into the intricacies of navigating the unpredictable landscape of real estate investment while mitigating risks and maximizing potential returns.

At its core, real estate investment involves a delicate balancing act between risk and reward. While the potential for lucrative returns can be enticing, investors must tread carefully and navigate the treacherous terrain of the market with caution and foresight. Understanding how to navigate this wild terrain requires a keen awareness of the various risks inherent in real estate investment and implementing strategies to mitigate them effectively.

One of the primary risks associated with real estate investment is market volatility. The real estate market is subject to fluctuations in supply and demand, economic conditions, and regulatory changes, all of which can impact property values and investment returns. Navigating this volatility requires diligent market research, thorough due diligence, and a deep understanding of macroeconomic trends and local market dynamics. By staying informed and proactive, investors can identify emerging opportunities and anticipate potential risks before they materialize.

Moreover, navigating the wild terrain of real estate investment involves assessing and managing property-specific risks. From physical risks such as structural defects or environmental hazards to financial risks such as tenant default or unexpected expenses, investors must conduct comprehensive risk assessments and implement risk mitigation strategies accordingly. This might involve conducting thorough property inspections, obtaining insurance coverage, or establishing contingency reserves to cover unforeseen expenses.

Another critical aspect of navigating the wild terrain of real estate investment is understanding and managing financing risks. Real estate transactions often involve significant capital investments, and investors must carefully consider the implications of leverage and debt financing on their investment portfolio. By maintaining a conservative approach to leverage, maintaining adequate liquidity reserves, and diversifying financing sources, investors can mitigate the risks associated with debt financing and safeguard their investment portfolio against adverse market conditions.

Furthermore, navigating the wild terrain of real estate investment requires a disciplined approach to portfolio management and asset allocation.

Diversification is key to mitigating risk and protecting against potential losses, and investors should spread their capital across a mix of property types, geographic locations, and investment strategies. By diversifying their portfolio, investors can reduce exposure to any single asset or market and cushion the impact of adverse market conditions on their overall investment performance.

In addition to proactive risk management strategies, successful navigation of the wild terrain of real estate investment also requires a mindset of resilience and adaptability. Despite diligent planning and risk mitigation efforts, unforeseen challenges and setbacks are inevitable in real estate investment. Investors must remain agile and responsive, adjusting their strategies and tactics in response to changing market conditions and unforeseen events. By embracing uncertainty and adversity as opportunities for growth and learning, investors can navigate the wild terrain of real estate investment with confidence and resilience.

In essence, navigating the wild terrain of real estate investment is a multifaceted endeavor that requires a combination of market expertise, risk management acumen, and resilience. By understanding the various risks inherent in real estate investment and implementing proactive risk mitigation strategies, investors can navigate the challenges of the market while maximizing potential returns. As we delve deeper into the chapters that follow, we will explore specific strategies and tactics for navigating the wild terrain of real estate investment and achieving success in this dynamic and rewarding industry.

Rule-Breaking Returns

In the world of real estate investment, conventional wisdom often dictates the strategies and tactics used to generate returns. However, this chapter, "Rule-Breaking Returns," challenges traditional norms and explores the innovative and unconventional methods that savvy investors employ to maximize profits in the dynamic landscape of real estate.

At its core, rule-breaking returns involve thinking outside the box and pushing the boundaries of conventional investment strategies. Rather than adhering strictly to established rules and practices, investors seek to disrupt the status quo and uncover new opportunities for generating outsized returns. This might involve leveraging alternative investment vehicles, exploring non-traditional asset classes, or implementing creative financing solutions to unlock hidden value in the market.

One rule-breaking method for maximizing profits in real estate is to embrace alternative investment vehicles such as real estate investment trusts (REITs), crowdfunding platforms, or real estate syndication. These innovative investment vehicles offer investors access to diversified portfolios of real estate assets without the need for direct ownership or management responsibilities. By diversifying their investment portfolio and accessing opportunities that may be out of reach for individual investors, participants can achieve attractive returns while mitigating risk.

Moreover, rule-breaking returns in real estate often involve exploring non-traditional asset classes and niche markets that offer unique opportunities for growth and profitability. This might include investing in specialized properties such as storage facilities, senior housing, or student housing, which have demonstrated resilience and strong demand drivers independent of broader market trends. By identifying underserved niches and capitalizing on emerging trends, investors can generate attractive returns while avoiding competition and market saturation.

Another rule-breaking method for maximizing profits in real estate is to implement creative financing solutions that leverage alternative sources of capital and minimize upfront investment requirements. This might involve structuring seller financing arrangements, utilizing lease options or land contracts, or tapping into private lending networks to secure flexible and favorable financing terms. By thinking creatively about financing options and structuring deals to optimize cash flow and returns, investors can unlock new opportunities for profitability and wealth creation.

Furthermore, rule-breaking returns in real estate often involve implementing unconventional strategies for property management and value enhancement. This might include leveraging technology and automation to streamline operations, implementing cost-saving measures to increase efficiency, or adopting innovative marketing tactics to attract and retain tenants. By embracing innovation and creativity in property management, investors can optimize performance, maximize cash flow, and enhance property values over time.

In essence, rule-breaking returns in real estate are about challenging the status quo and exploring new avenues for profitability and growth. By thinking outside the box, embracing innovation, and leveraging alternative investment vehicles, asset classes, and financing solutions, investors can unlock hidden value in the market and achieve superior returns. As we delve deeper into the chapters that follow, we will explore specific strategies and tactics for maximizing profits with out-of-the-box methods and achieving success in the dynamic and ever-evolving world of real estate investment.

Rebel Financing

In the realm of real estate investment, access to capital is often the key determinant of success. However, traditional financing options may not always be sufficient or suitable for every venture. This chapter, "Rebel Financing," explores the innovative and unconventional funding solutions that rebel investors employ to fuel their real estate ventures and achieve their financial goals.

At its core, rebel financing in real estate involves thinking outside the box and exploring alternative sources of capital beyond traditional bank loans or mortgage financing. Rather than relying solely on conventional funding methods, rebel investors seek out creative financing solutions that offer flexibility, speed, and favorable terms, allowing them to seize opportunities and maximize returns.

One rebel financing solution for real estate ventures is to leverage private lending networks or peer-to-peer lending platforms. These alternative financing sources provide investors with access to capital from individual investors or groups of investors who are willing to fund real estate projects in exchange for a favorable return on investment. By bypassing traditional financial institutions and tapping into private capital markets, investors can access funding quickly and on terms that are often more favorable than traditional bank loans.

Moreover, rebel investors may explore creative financing structures such as seller financing or lease options to acquire properties with minimal upfront capital requirements. Seller financing involves negotiating with the property seller to provide financing for the purchase, often in the form of a mortgage or installment sale agreement. Lease options allow investors to control a property through a lease agreement with an option to purchase at a later date, providing flexibility and upside potential without the need for a large initial investment.

Another rebel financing solution for real estate ventures is to utilize crowdfunding platforms to raise capital from a large pool of individual investors. Crowdfunding allows investors to pool their resources and collectively invest in real estate projects, typically through online platforms that facilitate the fundraising process. By harnessing the power of the crowd, investors can access capital quickly and efficiently, often with lower minimum investment requirements and greater transparency than traditional funding methods.

Furthermore, rebel financing in real estate may involve syndication or joint venture partnerships with other investors or industry professionals. Syndication involves pooling resources and expertise to jointly invest in larger real estate projects that may be beyond the scope of individual investors. Joint venture partnerships allow investors to collaborate with other stakeholders to share risks, resources, and rewards, leveraging collective strengths to achieve mutual goals.

In essence, rebel financing in real estate is about more than just securing funding for real estate ventures; it's about challenging the status quo and exploring new avenues for capital formation and investment. By thinking creatively, embracing alternative financing sources, and leveraging collaborative partnerships, investors can access the capital they need to fuel their real estate ventures and achieve their financial objectives. As we delve deeper into the chapters that follow, we will explore specific strategies and tactics for implementing rebel financing solutions and achieving success in the dynamic and competitive world of real estate investment.

Disruptive Development

In the ever-evolving landscape of real estate, traditional approaches to property development and management are being challenged by disruptive innovations that are reshaping the industry. This chapter, "Disruptive Development," explores the groundbreaking technologies, methodologies, and strategies that are revolutionizing property development and management, and the ways in which investors and developers can capitalize on these innovations to drive success.

At its core, disruptive development involves leveraging innovative technologies and methodologies to fundamentally transform the way properties are designed, constructed, operated, and managed. Rather than adhering to conventional practices, disruptors in the industry are embracing cutting-edge solutions that enhance efficiency, sustainability, and user experience, while unlocking new opportunities for value creation and differentiation.

One of the most significant innovations in property development is the adoption of advanced construction technologies such as modular construction, 3D printing, and robotics. These technologies enable developers to streamline the construction process, reduce costs, and accelerate project timelines, while also improving quality and precision. By embracing modular construction techniques, for example, developers can prefabricate building components off-site and assemble them on-site, resulting in faster construction times and lower labor costs.

Moreover, disruptive development is also characterized by the integration of smart building technologies and Internet of Things (IoT) devices into property design and management. Smart buildings leverage sensors, automation, and data analytics to optimize building performance, enhance energy efficiency, and improve occupant comfort and productivity. From intelligent lighting and HVAC systems to advanced security and access control solutions, smart building technologies are revolutionizing the way properties are operated and managed, while also reducing operational costs and environmental impact.

Another key innovation in property development is the rise of sustainable and eco-friendly building practices. With growing awareness of environmental issues and climate change, developers are increasingly prioritizing sustainability in their projects, incorporating green building materials, renewable energy sources, and energy-efficient design strategies. By embracing sustainable development practices, developers can not only reduce their environmental footprint but also appeal to environmentally conscious tenants and investors, while potentially lowering operating costs and enhancing long-term property value.

Furthermore, disruptive development is also reshaping the way properties are managed and operated, with the emergence of innovative property management platforms and software solutions. These platforms leverage data analytics, artificial intelligence, and machine learning to streamline property operations, improve tenant experiences, and optimize asset performance. From tenant communication and lease management to predictive maintenance and asset optimization, these technologies empower property managers to make data-driven decisions and drive operational efficiencies.

In essence, disruptive development in real estate is about more than just embracing new technologies; it's about fundamentally reimagining the way properties are designed, constructed, operated, and managed. By leveraging innovative construction techniques, smart building technologies, sustainable development practices, and advanced property management solutions, developers and investors can unlock new opportunities for value creation, differentiation, and success in the dynamic and competitive world of real estate. As we delve deeper into the chapters that follow, we will explore specific strategies and tactics for embracing disruptive development and achieving success in property development and management.

Renegade Networking

In the realm of real estate, success often hinges not only on what you know but also on who you know. This chapter, "Renegade Networking," delves into the art and science of building a powerhouse network in real estate, and how savvy investors and developers can leverage strategic relationships to unlock new opportunities, gain valuable insights, and achieve their financial goals.

Renegade networking in real estate is about more than just collecting business cards at industry events; it's about cultivating meaningful connections with like-minded professionals who can provide expertise, resources, and support. Rather than focusing solely on quantity, renegade networkers prioritize quality, seeking out individuals and organizations that share their values, goals, and vision for success in the industry.

One of the key principles of renegade networking is the concept of reciprocity. Renegade networkers understand that networking is a two-way street and prioritize building mutually beneficial relationships with their peers. By offering value, support, and assistance to others within their network, they create goodwill and foster a sense of camaraderie that strengthens their connections and enhances their reputation within the industry.

Moreover, renegade networking involves thinking outside the box and exploring unconventional avenues for building connections and expanding your network. While industry conferences and networking events can be valuable, renegade networkers understand that opportunities for networking exist everywhere, from social gatherings and community events to online forums and social media platforms. By staying open-minded and proactive, they seize every opportunity to connect with potential collaborators, mentors, and partners.

Another aspect of renegade networking is leveraging the power of strategic alliances and partnerships to amplify your reach and influence within the industry. Rather than going it alone, renegade networkers seek out synergistic relationships with complementary businesses and professionals who can provide access to new markets, resources, and opportunities. Whether it's forming joint ventures with other investors, collaborating with industry experts on educational initiatives, or partnering with service providers to offer value-added services, strategic alliances can be a powerful catalyst for growth and success in real estate.

Furthermore, renegade networking involves embracing diversity and inclusivity in your network, seeking out perspectives and experiences that differ from your own. By connecting with individuals from diverse backgrounds, cultures, and industries, renegade networkers can gain fresh insights, spark creativity, and identify new opportunities that may have been overlooked. In a rapidly changing and increasingly interconnected world, diversity is not only a moral imperative but also a strategic advantage that can drive innovation and foster resilience in the face of uncertainty.

In essence, renegade networking in real estate is about more than just building a rolodex of contacts; it's about cultivating authentic relationships, creating value, and fostering a sense of community within the industry. By prioritizing reciprocity, thinking outside the box, leveraging strategic alliances, and embracing diversity, renegade networkers can build a powerhouse network that empowers them to achieve their goals and thrive in the competitive world of real estate. As we delve deeper into the chapters that follow, we will explore specific strategies and tactics for mastering the art of renegade networking and unlocking new opportunities for success.

Rogue Renovations

Renovating properties is more than just a process of refurbishing and modernizing; it's an opportunity for creativity, innovation, and value enhancement. This chapter, "Rogue Renovations," delves into the unconventional and inventive tactics employed by renegade investors and developers to breathe new life into properties, maximize their potential, and achieve extraordinary returns.

Rogue renovations in real estate involve thinking outside the box and challenging conventional renovation practices to achieve distinctive and impactful transformations. Rather than following a one-size-fits-all approach, renegade renovators embrace creativity, resourcefulness, and ingenuity to reimagine properties in ways that set them apart from the competition and captivate buyers or tenants.

One unconventional tactic for rogue renovations is to focus on maximizing the property's unique character and charm. Rather than erasing all traces of the property's history, renegade renovators celebrate its heritage and architectural features, incorporating them into the design in creative and unexpected ways. Whether it's preserving original elements like exposed brick walls or reclaimed wood beams, or repurposing salvaged materials in innovative ways, embracing the property's unique character adds depth, authenticity, and charm to the renovation.

Moreover, rogue renovations often involve incorporating unconventional design elements and features that surprise and delight occupants. Renegade renovators aren't afraid to think outside the box and experiment with bold colors, textures, and materials to create spaces that evoke emotion and spark imagination. Whether it's installing eye-catching light fixtures, creating statement walls with unconventional materials, or incorporating unexpected architectural elements, rogue renovations challenge the status quo and push the boundaries of design innovation.

Another unconventional tactic for rogue renovations is to prioritize sustainability and eco-friendliness in the renovation process. Renegade renovators understand the importance of minimizing environmental impact and maximizing energy efficiency, and they integrate green building practices and sustainable materials into their renovations wherever possible. Whether it's installing energy-efficient appliances, incorporating passive design strategies to optimize natural lighting and ventilation, or using eco-friendly building materials such as reclaimed wood or recycled glass, sustainable renovations not only reduce the property's carbon footprint but also appeal to environmentally conscious buyers or tenants.

Furthermore, rogue renovations often involve reimagining the property's layout and functionality to better suit the needs and lifestyle of modern occupants. Renegade renovators aren't bound by conventional floor plans or design norms; they're willing to break down walls, rearrange spaces, and think creatively about how to maximize usability and flow. Whether it's converting underutilized spaces into multifunctional areas, creating open-concept living spaces, or incorporating flexible design elements that can adapt to changing needs, rogue renovations prioritize functionality and user experience above all else.

In essence, rogue renovations in real estate are about more than just updating properties; they're about infusing them with personality, purpose, and innovation. By embracing the property's unique character, incorporating unconventional design elements, prioritizing sustainability, and reimagining functionality, renegade renovators can transform ordinary properties into extraordinary spaces that stand out in the market and command premium prices. As we delve deeper into the chapters that follow, we will explore specific strategies and tactics for executing rogue renovations and achieving unparalleled success in property transformation

Underground Opportunities: Tapping into Hidden Gems in the Real Estate Market

In the vast and dynamic world of real estate, opportunities abound for those who know where to look. This chapter, "Underground Opportunities," uncovers the hidden gems and overlooked niches within the real estate market, and explores the strategies and tactics for tapping into these underground opportunities to unlock value and achieve success.

Underground opportunities in real estate are those that lie beneath the surface, hidden from plain sight and often overlooked by mainstream investors. These opportunities may exist in emerging markets, undervalued neighborhoods, or niche property types that have yet to attract widespread attention. By identifying and capitalizing on these hidden gems, investors can gain a competitive advantage and maximize their returns.

One strategy for tapping into underground opportunities is to focus on emerging markets and up-and-coming neighborhoods that have the potential for growth and revitalization. These areas may be overlooked by mainstream investors due to perceived risks or lack of visibility, but they often offer attractive investment prospects for those willing to take a calculated risk. By conducting thorough market research and due diligence, investors can identify emerging trends and opportunities before they become mainstream, positioning themselves to capitalize on future growth and appreciation.

Moreover, underground opportunities in real estate may also exist within niche property types or specialized market segments that are often overlooked by traditional investors. These could include properties such as self-storage facilities, mobile home parks, or mixed-use developments that cater to specific demographics or lifestyle preferences. By focusing on these niche markets, investors can avoid competition from mainstream investors and capitalize on untapped demand, achieving attractive returns with less risk.

Another strategy for uncovering underground opportunities is to leverage alternative sourcing channels and off-market deals. While many investors rely on publicly listed properties or listings from real estate agents, underground opportunities may be found through unconventional channels such as foreclosure auctions, distressed property sales, or direct marketing campaigns. By expanding their sourcing networks and staying alert to off-market opportunities, investors can gain access to hidden gems that others may overlook.

Furthermore, tapping into underground opportunities in real estate often requires a willingness to think creatively and adapt to changing market conditions. This may involve exploring innovative investment strategies or unconventional financing solutions to unlock value and maximize returns. Whether it's implementing a value-add strategy to renovate and reposition properties for higher rents or leveraging creative financing techniques such as seller financing or lease options, investors who are willing to think outside the box can uncover hidden opportunities for profit in the market.

In essence, underground opportunities in real estate represent a treasure trove of untapped potential for savvy investors who are willing to explore beyond the beaten path. By focusing on emerging markets, niche property types, alternative sourcing channels, and innovative investment strategies, investors can uncover hidden gems that others overlook and achieve exceptional returns in the dynamic and competitive world of real estate. As we delve deeper into the chapters that follow, we will explore specific strategies and tactics for identifying and capitalizing on underground opportunities to achieve success in real estate investment

Insurgent Negotiation

Negotiation lies at the heart of every successful real estate transaction, and mastering the art of negotiation is essential for achieving favorable outcomes and maximizing returns. This chapter, "Insurgent Negotiation," explores the bold and unconventional negotiation techniques employed by savvy investors and developers to secure advantageous deals and gain the upper hand in the competitive real estate market.

Insurgent negotiation in real estate involves thinking strategically, acting decisively, and challenging conventional negotiation norms to achieve desired outcomes. Rather than adopting a passive or reactive approach, insurgent negotiators proactively seize control of negotiations, leverage their strengths, and employ bold tactics to tip the scales in their favor.

One bold negotiation technique is to set ambitious yet achievable goals and anchor negotiations around these objectives. Insurgent negotiators understand the power of anchoring, and they strategically set the tone of negotiations by presenting bold offers or demands that serve as reference points for subsequent discussions. By anchoring negotiations at favorable terms, negotiators can influence perceptions of value and create momentum towards reaching their desired outcomes.

Moreover, insurgent negotiators are skilled at leveraging information asymmetry to their advantage and uncovering hidden leverage points that can be used to sway negotiations in their favor. Whether it's conducting thorough due diligence to uncover seller motivations or gathering market intelligence to identify comparable sales and rental rates, negotiators who are armed with valuable information can negotiate from a position of strength and gain concessions that may not have been otherwise possible.

Another bold negotiation technique is to employ persuasive and influential communication strategies to build rapport, establish trust, and persuade counterparts to agree to favorable terms. Insurgent negotiators understand the importance of effective communication in negotiations and tailor their messaging to appeal to the interests and motivations of the other party. Whether it's framing concessions as win-win solutions, using storytelling to evoke emotion, or employing assertive yet respectful language to convey confidence and authority, effective communication can be a powerful tool for influencing outcomes in negotiations.

Furthermore, insurgent negotiators are not afraid to walk away from the table if the terms of the deal are not favorable or if the other party is unwilling to negotiate in good faith. By demonstrating a willingness to walk away, negotiators signal to the other party that they are serious about their demands and that they have alternative options available. This can create a sense of urgency and compel the other party to reconsider their position, potentially leading to a more favorable outcome for the insurgent negotiator.

In essence, insurgent negotiation in real estate is about more than just haggling over price or terms; it's about seizing control of negotiations, leveraging strengths, and employing bold tactics to achieve desired outcomes. By setting ambitious goals, leveraging information asymmetry, employing persuasive communication strategies, and demonstrating a willingness to walk away, insurgent negotiators can gain the upper hand in negotiations and secure advantageous deals in the competitive real estate market. As we delve deeper into the chapters that follow, we will explore specific strategies and tactics for mastering the art of insurgent negotiation and achieving success in real estate transactions.

Legacy Building

Real estate ventures have the potential to transcend mere financial gain and leave a lasting legacy that extends far beyond the bottom line. This chapter, "Legacy Building," delves into the unconventional and transformative real estate ventures that go beyond traditional profit motives to create positive social, environmental, and cultural impact, leaving a lasting legacy for future generations.

Legacy building in real estate involves a mindset shift from short-term profitability to long-term sustainability and social responsibility. Rather than focusing solely on maximizing financial returns, legacy builders prioritize creating value that extends beyond the confines of individual transactions, leaving a positive imprint on communities, environments, and societies.

One avenue for legacy building in real estate is through the development of sustainable and environmentally conscious projects that prioritize ecological stewardship and resource conservation. Legacy builders embrace green building practices, incorporate renewable energy sources, and minimize environmental impact throughout the development process, creating buildings and communities that are not only resilient to climate change but also contribute to the overall health and well-being of residents and ecosystems.

Moreover, legacy builders seek to address pressing social and cultural challenges through innovative real estate ventures that promote inclusivity, diversity, and community empowerment. This might involve developing affordable housing initiatives, revitalizing blighted neighborhoods, or preserving historic landmarks and cultural heritage sites, creating spaces that foster social cohesion, economic opportunity, and cultural enrichment for residents and future generations.

Another avenue for legacy building in real estate is through the creation of mixed-use developments that integrate residential, commercial, and recreational elements to create vibrant, livable communities. Legacy builders understand the importance of place making and urban design in shaping the built environment and prioritize creating spaces that are walkable, accessible, and conducive to human interaction and well-being. By fostering a sense of belonging and community pride, mixed-use developments can become catalysts for positive social change and economic development.

Furthermore, legacy builders embrace unconventional real estate ventures that challenge the status quo and push the boundaries of traditional development models. This might include repurposing underutilized spaces for innovative uses, such as converting industrial warehouses into creative co-working spaces or transforming vacant lots into urban farms and green spaces. By reimagining the possibilities of the built environment, legacy builders can create opportunities for social innovation and positive transformation that leave a lasting impact on communities and societies.

In essence, legacy building in real estate is about more than just bricks and mortar; it's about creating spaces that enrich lives, strengthen communities, and leave a positive legacy for future generations. By embracing sustainability, social responsibility, and innovation, legacy builders can harness the transformative power of real estate to create a better, more equitable, and more resilient world. As we delve deeper into the chapters that follow, we will explore specific strategies and tactics for legacy building in real estate and the steps you can take to create a lasting impact through unconventional ventures.

Conclusion

"The Real Estate Renegade: Unconventional Tactics for Financial Freedom" has taken you on a journey through the dynamic and ever-evolving world of real estate, exploring innovative strategies, bold tactics, and transformative approaches that defy convention and redefine success. Throughout these pages, we've delved into the mindset of the renegade investor, the maverick developer, and the visionary builder, uncovering the secrets to unlocking hidden opportunities, maximizing profits, and leaving a lasting legacy in the world of real estate.

From breaking the mold with unconventional investment strategies to disrupting development practices with innovative technologies, from rogue renovations that breathe new life into properties to insurgent negotiation tactics that secure favorable deals, this book has equipped you with the knowledge, skills, and mindset needed to thrive in the competitive and dynamic real estate market.

But beyond the pursuit of financial gain, "The Real Estate Renegade" has also emphasized the importance of creating value that extends beyond the bottom line – value that enriches lives, strengthens communities, and leaves a positive legacy for future generations. Whether it's through sustainable development practices, socially responsible investment initiatives, or innovative place making efforts, the renegade investor understands that true success lies in making a meaningful and lasting impact in the world.

As you embark on your journey as a real estate renegade, remember that the path to financial freedom is not always smooth or straightforward. It requires courage, creativity, and resilience to navigate the challenges and uncertainties of the market, and the willingness to challenge the status quo and embrace the unconventional.

So, dare to break the mold, think outside the box, and forge your own path to success in real estate. Be bold, be innovative, and above all, be a renegade – and watch as you transform not only your own financial future but also the world around you. Here's to your success as a real estate renegade.

www.ingramcontent.com/pod-product-compliance
Lightning Source LLC
Chambersburg PA
CBHW070355230526
45471CB00006B/2580